THE HOLY SACRIFICE
OF THE MASS

THE
HOLY SACRIFICE
OF THE MASS

Very Rev. Martin B. Hellriegel

Os Justi Press

Nihil Obstat
William Fischer, s.t.d.
Censor Librorum

Imprimatur
✠ John J. Glennon, s.t.d.
Archbishop of St. Louis
September 1, 1944

The Holy Sacrifice of the Mass was first published in 1944
by Pio Decimo Press, Saint Louis, Missouri.
The present book is a reproduction of the 1945 printing.
The work is in the public domain.

Os Justi Press
P.O. Box 21814
Lincoln, NE 68542
www.osjustipress.com

Send inquiries to
info@osjustipress.com

ISBN 978-1-965303-55-9 (paperback)
ISBN 978-1-965303-58-0 (hardcover)

Cover design by Julian Kwasniewski

Dedicated
To my Father in Christ
The Most Reverend John Joseph Glennon, S.T.D.
who on the Thirtieth Anniversary of His Ordination
to the Priesthood of Christ, December 20th, 1914,
made me a Minister of Christ and Dispenser of the
Mysteries of God.
Gratefully and Wholeheartedly
I shall renew to my Father my Obedience and Reverence
On December 20th, 1944
The Blessed Day of His Diamond Jubilee as Priest
of the Most High God.

His son in Christ
M. B. H.

CONTENTS

AUTHOR'S PREFACE

During the "School of Liturgy" held at Mundelein Seminary in 1941, and again during Lent of 1942 at his parish church of "The Holy Cross," St. Louis, Mo., the author spoke on the topic "The Holy Sacrifice of the Mass." When the editors of "The Living Parish" (Pio Decimo Press) asked him to write a series of articles on this subject, a subject dear to every Catholic heart, he could not refuse.

Vol. III and IV, therefore, of "The Living Parish" contained these articles which (except for a few minor changes) appear here in book form. The reader will find several rather extensive quotations from the precious booklet "Sacred Signs" by Dr. Romano Guardini. A threefold reason prompted the author to insert these quotations: Firstly, their unusual vigor in showing forth the symbolic meaning of sacred words and signs. Perhaps no one before has seen more clearly "the soul behind the body" than Guardini. Secondly, to direct the attention of readers to the booklet "Sacred Signs," which, in the United States, may not have received the attention it so well deserves. Thirdly, in grateful remembrance of the fine liturgical work done by Father Guardini who from 1912 – 13 was assistant at the author's home parish at Heppenheim, diocese of Mainz. The author is deeply indebted to the publishers of "Sacred Signs," Sheed and Ward, England, for the use of these quotations.

If the contents of this book "The Holy Sacrifice of the Mass" will awaken in the reader a greater love for the Holy Eucharist and a more active and soulful participation in the daily re-presentation of the mystery of the Cross, the author will feel that God has blessed his work.

Feast of the Exaltation of the
    Holy Cross
    September 14th, 1944   M. B. H.

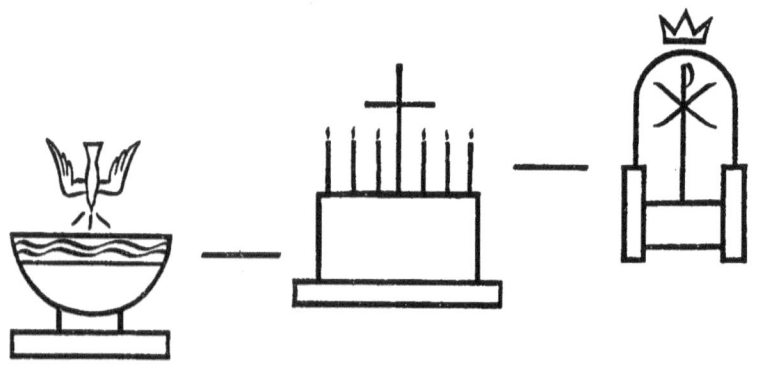

INTRODUCTION

I.

FONT AND ALTAR

THE holiest places on earth are the baptismal font and the eucharistic altar. The first is the virginal, immaculate womb of Mother Church from which we were born "out of water and the Holy Ghost." The other is the sacred spot on which the Man-God, Christ the Lord, makes present His Sacrifice of Calvary for the glory of the Father and the redemption of mankind. Font and altar — HER place and HIS place — are worthy of the greatest respect and love by priest and people. At the first we were born. At the second we, God's children, give our highest homage to our Father and are nourished by Him with the Flesh and Blood of His Son, so that we may grow from spiritual babes unto the measures of the fulness of Christ.

On our baptismal day the Church clothed us with the white garment, saying: "Receive this white garment and carry it without spot to the Judgment Seat of our Lord Jesus Christ."

II.

THE ROYAL HIGHWAY

A tremendous line! A most holy road! The highway on which a Christian must march from earth to heaven! This highway leads over the altar. Ordinarily, no Christian (a Christian is another Christ) who has attained the use of reason can reach the "Judgment Seat of our Lord Jesus Christ" without going over the altar, for "unless you eat the Flesh of the Son of Man and drink His Blood, you shall not have life in you." Font and altar! Once more we repeat: Priest and flock owe profoundest reverence to these two sacred places. One eye must ever be focused on the altar, the other on the font. We can not treasure the one without loving the other. The more we understand the sublime purpose of the font, the more we will value the divine purpose of the altar.

Some time ago the great liturgical leader Dr. Pius Parsch gave an instruction to a group of children ranging from 3 to 6 years, in which he emphasized that baptism does not merely remove original sin, but that in baptism we are *born* to the life of God. Among these children was a little fellow of 5 whose mother had just been blessed with another boy.

A few days later an uncle arrived (to be god-father at the baptism). "Philip," asked the uncle, "when was your little brother born?" To which the 5 year old nephew replied: "Uncle, he isn't born yet, he will be born next Sunday."

III.

THE SUN

The holy Eucharist is the Sun of our Christian life. Every day, three hundred and sixty-five times in the year, the sun of *nature* rises, ever the same, yet ever new; daily unfolding his brightness and warmth, daily producing new effects in *all* on which he shines. So it is with the eucharistic Sun. Three hundred and sixty-five times in the "Year of Salvation" He rises, ever the same, yet ever new, daily manifesting His brightness and warmth, daily imparting new vitality and growth to the "branches" grafted on Him, the "Vine," at the font of Baptism. "The Bread that I will give you is my Flesh for the LIFE of the world." We live *by* the Eucharist, and must live *for* the Eucharist. Without It "you shall not have LIFE in you." The life of every Christian must therefore be Eucharistico-centric.

In the center: The Sun, the Holy Sacrifice of the Mass (1). Surrounding it, the big stars, the sacraments (2): The star of *Baptism* with its Christ-carrying waters; the star of *Confirmation* with the Spirit-filled chrism; the star of *Penance* with the Easter-peace of the risen Lord: the star of *Extreme Unction* with its two rays — one pointing to restoration "of former health and joyful service in the Church," the other to final consecration of the last portion of our earthly pilgrimage; the next star — the one so magnificently illumined by the eucharistic Sun — *Holy Orders*, sending forth its golden rays of spiritual paternity: and the star of *Matrimony* with the silver rays of natural paternity. — Behind the big stars, the little stars,

the sacramentals, the "little" sacraments (3). Behind them the vials (4) with the incense of the Church's prayers. Finally those innumerable duties pertaining to parochial life (5), sodality, society work, finances, and (6) those many other things that could quite well be done by non-consecrated hands, but are being done by priests, either because lay-folk show themselves unwilling, or because priests have failed to train the people to take a more active part in the various social activities — (baseball, bowling, bazaars and what not, these more or less 'necessary' affairs in our present day parochial set-up).

What a pity, if our attention would primarily circle about things secondary, instead of coming from, and moving back to the divinely established center, the eucharistic Sun. To depart from this Christ-willed order would spell failure. In the end we would be compelled to say with St. Peter: "We have fished all night and . . . ."

IV.

TWO MOMENTOUS QUESTIONS AND ANSWERS

"Wilt thou be baptized?" is the first and most important of all questions that can be placed before a human being. "I will" was the answer. And we were born to God; became living branches of Christ the Vine.

The *other* question is of equal importance: "What is the Holy Sacrifice of the Mass?" Every Christian is bound to answer also this question, not simply in words, but by a eucharistic life, by *offering* himself with the eucharistic Lord to God the Father, and by *receiving* from the Father the sacrificed Flesh and Blood of the Son. Says the Secret of the Ninth Sunday after Pentecost: "As often as this *Saving Victim* is offered up, so often is the work of redemption enacted." As often as Holy Mass is offered, so often is the redeeming work of Christ made present for the glory of God and for the salvation of men of good will. By the "work of redemption" is meant all that our holy Redeemer has done and will do down to His last coming in power and majesty.

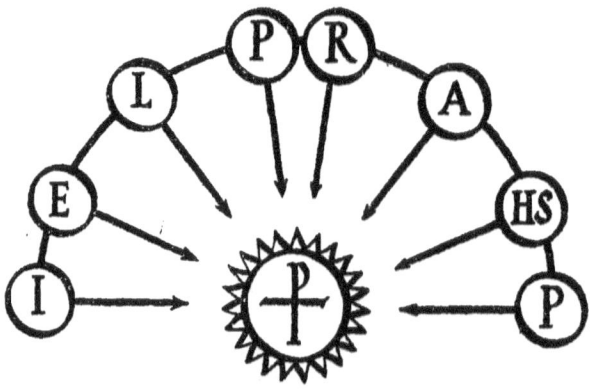

SAVING VICTIM

I. His Incarnation, E. His Epiphany, L. His Life, hidden and public, P. R. His Passion-Resurrection, A. His Ascension, HS. the Sending of His Holy Spirit and P. His Parousia, His victorious return at the end of time. The "Saving Victim" is none other than the eternal Logos, the Word-made-Man, whose acts are indivisible. Therefore, whenever He steps out of eternity into time — as He does in every Holy Mass — He comes with all that He did, does and will do.

The climax of the "work of redemption" is the mystery of Calvary, the life-giving death of Jesus Christ. All other events in His life either lead up to it or flow from it. Morning after morning the Church reminds us that the whole "Work of Redemption" is present on the altar. "Wherefore, O Lord, we Thy servants (the priests) and likewise Thy holy people (the faithful) are *mindful* of the blessed Passion of the same Christ Thy Son, our Lord, and also of His Resurrection from the dead and of His glorious Ascension nto heaven ..." "Mindful," not only *subjectively* — by way of devout remembering — but *objectively*, because there is actually before us the entire work of redemption. It is of interest to note that in by-gone days also he "Epiphany" (before "blessed Passion") and the "Parousia" (after "glorious Ascension") were mentioned.

A realization of this sublime truth must fill us with profound awe and reverence, and bring about an increasing love for the eucharistic mystery of the altar — and that will be our best answer to the question: "What is the Holy Sacrifice of the Mass?"

Through Baptism — Through the Holy Eucharist

Part One

THE FORE-MASS

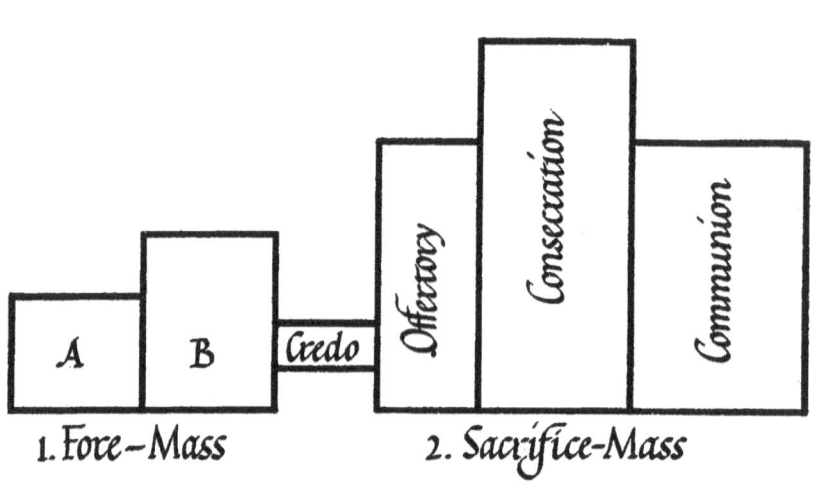

1. Fore–Mass   2. Sacrifice-Mass

CHAPTER ONE
PRAYER

OUR "customary" way of dividing Holy Mass into "three *principal* parts: Offertory, Consecration and Communion" is by no means fortunate. What about that part which precedes the Offertory? An over-emphasis of "principal" parts will make the preceding part seem rather "secondary." Are the prayers, the lesson and the holy Gospel of Jesus Christ which precede the Offertory really "secondary?" Would it not be more correct to say: Ho y Mass consists of *two principal* parts, viz. 1) The Fore-Mass and 2) The Sacrifice-Mass? This division is complete and will make us realize that the Fore-Mass is part and parcel of Holy Mass, and will warn those who on Sundays and days of obligation come as late as up "to the three principal parts", that it is wrong to intentionally miss that part of the Mass whose purpose is to prepare the whole man, mind, heart and body, for a worthy celebration of the sacrifice of our redemption. The two diagrams (pages 20 and 22) will help to illustrate our explanation.

Part I consists of *two* sections: A. Prayer and B. Instruction. Let us consider section after section. The "prayer-section" contains four distinct elements, four distinct motifs,—two, as it were, in a *minor*, and two in a *major* key.

The first two (1 and 2) stress the *need of redemption*. "Lord, we have sinned against Thee, have mercy on us!" The other two (3 and 4) assure us that *we are redeemed*, that we may call God "Abba, Father, through Jesus Christ His Son our Lord." The four motifs are: 1. Sorrow, 2. Longing, 3. Praise, 4. Petition. These four elements are contained in what we call: The Prayer Service.

Let us now make a brief study of line 1 (sorrow). The celebrant begins Holy Mass "at the *foot* of the altar." If a priest desires to be truly great on the predella he must be truly small at the foot of the altar. Servers and people kneel. How significant! Yet so often we do things mechanically, thoughtlessly. Here he stands, at the *foot* of the altar, the father of God's family, in sorrow and humility, like the Publican "who was justified" because he "stood" so well.

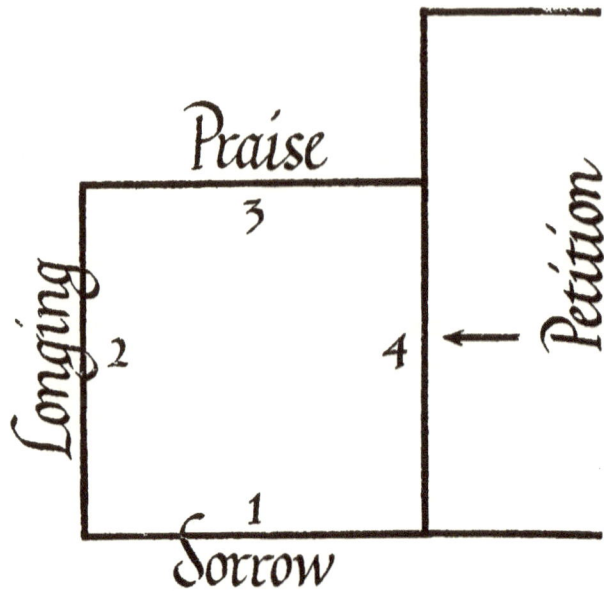

Here he must publicly confess his wrongs before God and the entire mystic Christ. There they kneel, servers and people, like the Magdalen at the foot of the Cross with contrition and grief, so that much may be forgiven them because they loved much. "An humble and contrite heart Thou, O God, wilt not despise."

Now we sign ourselves with the sign of redemption, with the sign of faith in the Holy Trinity. Says Romano Guardini (in *Sacred Signs*, translated by G. C. H. Pollen, S. J.) "You make the sign of the Cross, and make it rightly. Nothing in the way of hasty waving of the hand, from which no one could understand what you are doing — no, a real sign of the Cross, slow, large from forehead to breast, and from one shoulder to the other. Don't you feel that it takes in the whole of you? Gather up all thoughts and feelings into this sign, as it goes from forehead to breast; pull yourself together, as it goes from shoulder to shoulder. It covers the whole of you, body and soul; it gathers you up, dedicates you, sanctifies you. Why? Because it is the sign of the whole man and the sign of redemption. On the Cross our Lord redeemed all men. Through the Cross He sanctified the whole man, to the very last fibre of his being.

"That is why we cross ourselves *before* our prayers, so that the sign may pull us together and set us in order, may fix thoughts, heart and will in God. *After* prayers we cross ourselves, so that what God has given us may stay with us. In temptation, that it may strengthen us; in danger, that it may protect us; when a blessing is given, that the fulness of life from God may be taken into our soul and may consecrate all in it and make it fruitful. Think of this when you make the sign of the cross. It is the holiest sign there is. Make it carefully, slowly; make a large one, with recollection. For then it embraces your whole being, body and soul, your thoughts and your will, imagination and feeling, doing and resting; and in it all will be strengthened, stamped, consecrated in the power of Christ, in the name of the Holy Trinity."

"In nomine Patris et Filii et Spiritus Sancti," so we begin, at the *foot* of the altar, at the foot of the mystic Calvary, at the foot of the earthly throne of heaven's Trinity.

1. SORROW. THE CONFITEOR

I shall never forget an instruction on the "Confiteor" given to

children by Dr. Pius Parsch: God is seated on His throne of glory, surrounded by the most blessed Virgin Mary, blessed Michael, leader of the heavenly army, blessed John the Baptist, royal precursor of the Lamb of God, the illustrious princes Saints Peter and Paul, and all the saints (s) . . . . .

Here he stands ('), the shepherd; there they kneel ('''''''), his flock, each one confessing "I have sinned much in thought, word and deed, through my fault, through my fault, through my most grievous fault." What now? Realizing my unworthiness to appeal to God's awe-inspiring majesty for pardon, I ask the glorious Mother of God, St. Michael and all the citizens of the celestial Jerusalem "to intercede *for me* before the Lord our God." "Ask and you shall receive!" From the high and merciful throne comes the answer: "Pardon, absolution and remission" to all, priest and people.

The "prodigal" is now reconciled with the Father. Innocent in hands and clean of heart the celebrant ascends unto the holy Mount, the eucharistic Calvary, and with him in spirit the faithful. He places his hands on the altar,—"the Altar is Christ" (Roman Pontifical) — kisses it, kisses Him, Christ, and through Him the Father and, receives from the Father through Christ the kiss of friendship, of sonship, of life and of love.

From time to time an instruction should be given in church and school on the meaning and holiness of the altar (stone). Many Catholics go through life without ever seeing an altar stone, the

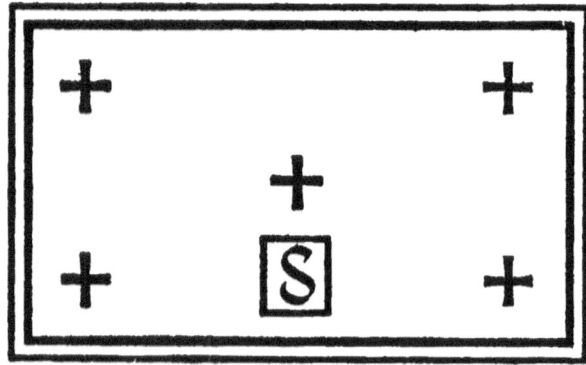

consecrated stone on which lifeless bread is changed into the Bread of Life. Some years ago the writer found an altar stone wrapped in a "funny paper." "The altar is Christ!" "Comics" had *doubly* become "tragics." When explaining the altar stone take the sacred stone with you, but place it on a white cloth, not just anywhere. "*Sancta sancte!*" Treat holy things in a holy manner!

In the stone is a small hallowed sepulchre (S) containing relics of some of Christ's triumphant athletes. "Where I am there my minister also shall be." Fruitful branches, intimately united with the Blessed Vine! Eight times during Holy Mass the celebrant kisses the sacred stone — Christ, the Vine, and the relics of His martyrs, His branches, thereby bringing his own love and homage, and that of his flock, to Vine and branches, to Head and members, to the great Christ, the whole Christ, the mystic Christ. Do holy things in a holy manner!

Now the priest recites the Introit, the entrance anthem, which however is *outside* the motifs we are speaking of. Originally it was not said by the celebrant. It was sung by the choir. The early Church avoided needless repetitions. With the introduction of "low Mass" it became customary (it was no happy move) to recite also in the high (solemn high, pontifical) Mass those portions which were rendered by the chanters (or read and sung by subdeacon and deacon). Originally the Introit was the processional chant accompanying the solemn entrance of the clergy through the church to the altar. But because the way to the altar has been considerably shortened, its main purpose today is to awaken in clergy and faithful those sentiments of faith and love necessary for the mystery they are about to celebrate in Christian fellowship. The Introit is the overture, the key, to the feast. What heart can remain untouched by the sublime words and the even more sublime music of the "To Thee, O Lord, I lift up my soul" on the first day of the Church's new year? Or the "A Child is born to us, a Son is given to us" on the day of the Lord's birth, or the "I arose and am still with Thee, alleluja" on the day which the Lord has made, or "The Spirit of the Lord has filled the whole earth, alleluja" on the feast of Pentecost?

2. LONGING. THE KYRIE (LORD, HAVE MERCY)

Reconciled with the triune God by an humble "Confiteor" we now turn to Him and cry out: "Kyrie, Christe, Kyrie eleison." Three times each. Nine times in all. A ninefold acclamation to our great God. A ninefold plea also for mercy. Does not the Gospel of the Rogation days come to our mind as we recite the Kyrie? "Yet if he shall continue knocking, I say to you although he will not rise and give him because he is his friend; yet because of his importunity he will rise and give him as many as he needeth."

Kyrie, Kyrie, Kyrie! How the Church loves to make use of the 'principle of gradation.' A few remarks about that. Think of the unveiling of the cross on Good Friday. From a low place, in a low tone, and a partial uncovering — to the high place, in a high tone

— 25 —

and the full unveiling! No Christian heart can remain untouched by this gradation. No one is able to preach a sermon as soul-stirring as this triple action will preach. Or think of the grandest gradation, that on Holy Saturday, when the paschal candle is inserted into the Font, deep, deeper and still deeper, the while the officiating priest chants high, higher and still higher: "May the power of the Holy Ghost descend into all the water of this Font." A gradation in *two* directions — down and up — three times. Surely, grace is poured out upon thy lips, O Holy Church of God, by the Spirit of the Lord that worketh in thee!

Kyrie, Christe, Kyrie. An ardent desire to be with God, a fervent plea for help and mercy. This second motif is followed by the *third* (3 Pr), that of praise. The first and second are like a *minor* chord,

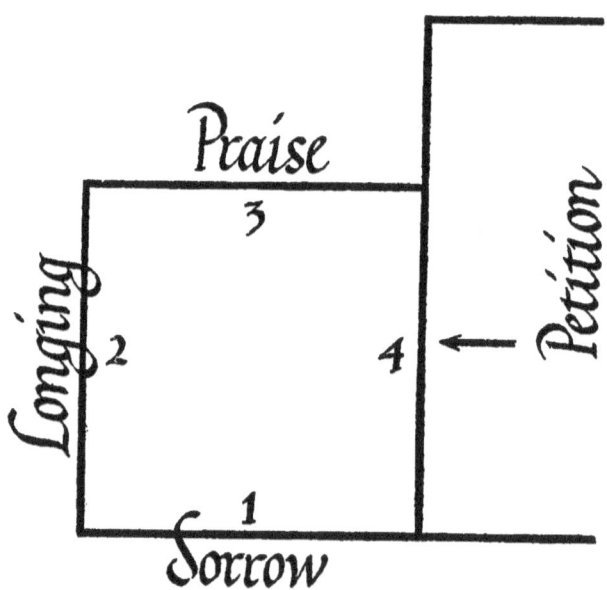

"I am a sinner, I am in need of redemption." The third, a *major*, is already permeated with joy and gladness, "I have found God my Father."

3. PRAISE. THE GLORIA

The "Gloria," the angelic hymn, was born when the King of angels was born. Composed by the Holy Spirit, sung by the angels, completed by the Church! It is the Church's morning hymn to Father, Son and Holy Ghost. "Lord, God, heavenly King, God, the *Father* almighty."—"O Lord God, Lamb of God, *Son* of the Father."—"With the *Holy Ghost* in the glory of God the Father."

"Glory to God, Peace to men!" All is contained in these few words. Could the angels have announced more? The purpose of our Savior's coming was precisely this: "To give glory to God, and Peace to men." Such was *His* work, such is the *Church's* work, such is the work of *every* one of her members.

This angelic hymn must never be said with unangelic mumbling. The "Greater Doxology," as the Greeks call the Gloria, wants to be treated with awe and reverence; with, at least, a spark of that enthusiasm wherewith the angels first chanted it over the fields of Bethlehem and now say it with us in the "house of Bread" of our parish (or convent) church.

4. PETITION. THE COLLECT

The climax of the "Prayer-Service" is the Collect (4-P), that particular portion which unites beautifully the Mass and divine Office. *Once* the Collect is said in the holy Sacrifice and *five* times in the *office*. What a glorious picture! Three hundred and seventy-five thousand priests saying daily *one time* plus *five times* the official solemn prayer of the Church, presenting their own intentions and those of three hundred and sixty million faithful by this prayer "through Jesus Christ our Lord, God's Son" to the Father in heaven!

Sometimes we hear people say "oration." But the Latin "oratio and our English "oration" are not the same thing. "Collect," I think, is a better word. On "stational days" it was customary for the clergy and faithful to assemble in the "ecclesia *collecta*." When all were together, and before the procession to the stational church began the pope sang the "collecta." Then, chanting the litany of the saints, catechumens, penitents, faithful, clergy and pontiff proceeded to the station to celebrate with Sabina, John and Paul, Cecilia, Lawrence the eucharistic mystery. Hence "collect." But "collect" also because the celebrant — the father of God's family — *collects* all the intentions and aspirations of his children. —The total assembly of *faithful, penitents* and *catechumens* was called "ecclesia *collecta*." The faithful who, after the dismissal of catechumens and penitents, remained for the eucharistic solemnity constituted the "ecclesia *secreta* (segregata)." When finally these were dismissed by the

"Ite missa est" we had the "ecclesia (dim) *missa.*" Collecta, secreta (dim) missa.

The Collects are full of the "sober inebriety of the Spirit." That is possibly one of the main reasons why our "emotional age" can not "stomach" (as someone remarked) these prayers of the Church. Many prefer spiritual angel-cake to divine whole-wheat bread. Many years ago, when Father Lasance's first English missal made its appearance, I gave a copy to a good, pious lady who had done much for the altar, believing that thereby I had made "quite a nice contribution" towards the furthering of the apostolate begun by Pius X. Several weeks later this good lady told me: "I can't thank you enough for the missal you gave me, Father. Oh, there are some wonderful prayers in the *back* of that book."

The following diagram illustrates the structure of the Collect.

I.	INTRODUCTION:	Oremus (*let us pray*)!
II.	ADDRESS:	O God,
III.	REASON:	who by the humility of Thy Son hast raised up a fallen world,
IV.	PETITION:	grant to Thy faithful people abiding joy,
V.	FRUIT:	that those whom Thou hast delivered from the perils of eternal death, Thou mayest cause to enjoy endless happiness.
VI.	CONCLUSION:	Through the same Jesus Christ Thy Son our Lord . . . Amen.

All the elder Collects are addressed to *God the Father.* That was the early Church's way of thinking. To God the Father through the Mediator Jesus Christ. "Amen, amen, I say to you: If you ask the Father anything in My name, He will give it you." Some of the younger Collects are directed to the Son. No Collect in the missal is addressed to the Holy Ghost. But whether directed to the Father or to the Son, practically every Collect closes with a solemn confession of the Blessed Trinity.

And now a few suggestions: 1. To our teachers and professors of high school, college, minor and major seminary: Instead of using before class, year in, year out, the same (often mechanically recited) form of prayer, why not use the Church's "Collect of the day?" Varietas delectat! It would create a fine "sentire cum Ecclesia, living with the Church," and at the same time be a spiritual and intellectual gain for everybody. We follow this plan in our grade school. 2. To my confreres: We are so familiar with the "Oremus" and the "Per Dominum nostrum Jesum Christum" that we are apt to go through them hurriedly and superficially. And yet, are they not the most sacred part of the Collect? "Oremus," — now, just a moment of silence, — then continue. And the "Per Dominum-nostrum," what momentous words! We must say them slowly, and with faith and dignity. The majesty of our Mediator in whose name we petition the Father demands that. 3. To the faithful: You conclude the Collect. "Amen" you say, "so be it." It is your privilege as "the chosen generation and kingly priesthood" to confirm and conclude what the anointed leader spoke at God's altar. As Mass goes on you will do so again at the end of the Offertory and at the conclusion of the Canon. Do not forget the privilege that is yours. "Be not a silent onlooker" as Pius XI said, but take an active part. "Amen." So be it!

And so we come to the end of the first portion of the Fore-Mass, the "Prayer Service." Man has spoken to God. It is now his duty to be quiet and let God speak to him. O wonderful interchange! Man speaks and God speaks. How do you proceed when you call on — let us say — your bishop? First, you wipe the dust off your shoes, secondly, you ring his doorbell, thirdly, you greet him and lastly, you place your petition before him. That is all. Now it is the bishop's turn to speak to you, If he offers you a chair you will sit down and listen attentively. We do precisely the same when we go to God, "the bishop of our souls." In the "Confiteor" we wipe off the dust from our soul; in the "Kyrie Christe, Kyrie" we ring the doorbell of God's heart; in the "Gloria" we greet our God, and in the "Collect" we place our petition before Him "through Jesus Christ His Son our Lord." We have said everything. We now sit down and await God's answer,

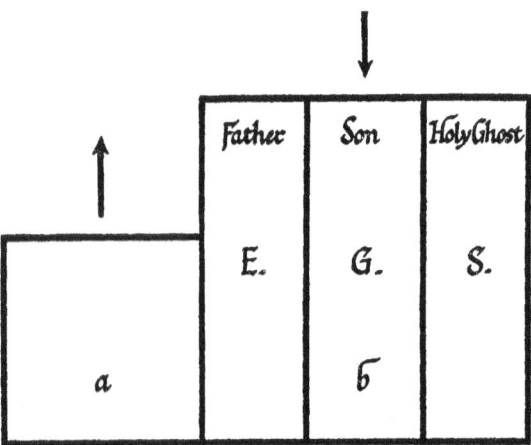

a. Man speaks to God. *b.* God speaks to Man.

CHAPTER TWO

INSTRUCTION

1. THE EPISTLE. THE FATHER SPEAKS

Now it is God's turn to speak. Three messages He sends us, the Epistle, the Gospel and the Sermon. Not in vain did we ring three times at the merciful heart of our God: "Kyrie, Christe, Kyrie." From each Person of the Blessed Trinity we receive an answer. The *Father* speaks, not personally, but through an ambassador, either of the Old or of the New Testament. The *Son* Himself speaks in the Gospel. The *Holy Spirit* speaks through His anointed mouthpiece, the priest.

It is interesting to note that on Sundays the Epistle is *always* taken from the *New* Testament. Every Sunday is a continuation of Easter Sunday, and Easter is the beginning of the eternal Newness. "Recedent vetera, nova sint omnia, let olden things depart, let all be new." On other days the Epistle may be from the Old or from the New Testament. The Old Testament reading is usually introduced by "hæc dicit Dominus, thus saith the Lord." From these three words one can almost sense the origin of the message. But when it begins "carissimi, dearly beloved" we can expect to listen to St. John, the disciple of love. And when it says "fratres, brethren" we can almost be certain that our big brother St. Paul, master of the "brotherhood in Christ," is addressing us.

With attention and reverence we listen to the Epistle and, at the end, extend a sincere "Deo gratias, thanks to God" who a) encouraged us by the heroism of some great sons and daughters of Israel; or who b) replenished our minds by the words of wisdom; or who c) revealed to us the love and generosity of the Vine's first branches — as recorded in the Acts; or who d) enlightened our understanding by the heavenly doctrines contained in the letters of the Apostles; or who, after casting aside the veil of time, e) permitted us to behold the glory of the celestial Jerusalem where angels and ancients, saints and elect cry out unceasingly: "Salvation to our God who sitteth upon the throne and to the Lamb." Deo gratias! Thanks to our God for such messages of encouragement and light!

The Epistle is followed by the Gradual, the chant which has two "faces," one looking *backward* to the message just received from the Father, imploring Him that His word fall like good seed on the soil of our soul; the other, looking *forward*, to "the coming of the Blessed Hope, our Savior Jesus Christ," who is about to appear in our midst to speak to us words of eternal life.

Very delicately do the Alleluja-verses prepare us for the "Tidings of great joy." For example, on the Ninth Sunday after Pentecost: "Alleluja, alleluja, deliver me from my enemies, O my God." And the Gospel: ". . . and thy enemies shall cast a trench about thee." The Tenth Sunday: "Alleluja, alleluja. To *Thee*, O God, we must sing in Sion, to *Thee* a vow shall be paid in Jerusalem." And the Gospel: ". . . two men went up to pray, the one a pharisee, and the other a publican," the one singing proudly his own merits, the other paying humbly the vow of gratitude to the God of mercy.

2. THE HOLY GOSPEL. THE SON SPEAKS

Before announcing the Gospel the priest recites the "Munda *cor* meum ac *labia* mea," the prayer which sanctifies *heart* and *lips* for a worthy proclamation of the most holy word of Jesus Christ. "Cleanse my heart and my lips, O almighty God, who didst cleanse the lips of the prophet Isaias with a burning coal; vouchsafe through Thy gracious mercy so to cleanse me that I may worthily proclaim Thy holy Gospel."

In order to appreciate the full meaning of the "glad Tidings that shall be to all the people" we must remember that the ideal form of celebrating the Mass is the Solemn Highmass, not the chanted Mass, and certainly not the "low" Mass. In the Solemn Highmass the deacon places the Gospel book on the Altar. "The Altar is Christ" says the Roman Pontifical. From the Altar, from Christ, comes the life-giving word. Before the Altar the deacon kneels, praying for purification of heart and lips and begging the blessing of the celebrating priest (in whom Christ, the Highpriest, is present) "that I may worthily proclaim His holy Gospel." "May the Lord be in thy heart and on thy lips, that thou mayest meetly and fitly announce His Gospel. In the name of the Father and of the Son and of the Holy Ghost," replies the celebrant. The deacon now carries the sacred book towards the faithful, holding it not before his breast as the subdeacon did with the "book of the epistles," but lifted up so as to hide his face and to magnify and extol the "Word of Christ and Christ, the Word." It is the "Verbum Christi" that matters! (Sometimes people are more interested in the minister proclaiming the word of Christ than in the word of Christ proclaimed by His minister.) Amid clouds of blessed incense and lighted candles the deacon (with the Lord in his heart and on his lips) announces the "Tidings of great joy that shall be to all the people," tidings which fill our soul with the odor of Christ's sweetness and our minds with the light of truth and life. We stand. Standing means preparedness. But let us listen again to Guardini: "Standing signifies, above all, that we pull ourselves together; instead of the slack position of sitting, we take a stiff, controlled attitude. It means that we are attentive. We are, as soldiers say, "at attention." Standing has in it something of stress, of watchfulness. It shows that we are ready. He who stands can immediately go off here and there; he can undertake any task without delay; he can begin any work as soon as he is shown what to do.

"This is the other side of reverence for God. We *kneel* when we want to pray, to rest before God. Here we are ready for action. This is the reverence of the attentive servant, of the armed warrior. They show their readiness. We *stand* when the joyful good news is intoned from the altar at the Gospel during Mass. Godparents *stand* at baptism when they make the solemn declaration of faith in the name of the child. We all *stand* when we renew these promises at a Mission. Bridegroom and bride *stand* before the altar when they pledge their troth in marriage. There are many other examples which you will observe yourselves. Even when a man is alone, it may often fit his inner state if he prays *standing*. The early Christians were fond of this position. There is a well-known picture in the Catacombs of a female figure in nobly flowing robes, standing with outstretched arms, a picture of freedom with clear self-control, of silent attention to the word and joyous readiness to act.

"Sometimes we feel as if we could not pray kneeling — as if it cramped us. Then to *stand* will free us from that feeling, and will do us good. But it must be the right kind of *standing*. On both feet, with straight knees and back, not leaning against anything, upright and full of self-control. Then our prayer also comes under control and is yet free, in reverence and readiness."

"Dominus vobiscum, the Lord be with you!" "Sequentia sancti Evangelii secundum Matthæum, (Marcum, Lucam, Joannem)." We answer: "Gloria Tibi, Domine, Glory be to Thee, Lord." Why do we say "Tibi, to Thee?" Unless the Lord were present, would it not be strange to say "to Thee?" The Church is so convinced that the Blessed Christ, gloriously sitting at the right hand of the Father, is "hic et nunc" mystically, but truly present to speak to us words of eternal life that she asks us to welcome Him joyfully: "Gloria, Tibi, Domine" and, at the end, to thank Him for His words of life by a wholehearted: "Laus Tibi, Christe, praise be to Thee, O Christ." Let us not forget Guardini's warning: "We are living in an age of signs and words and understand no longer their meaning."

We sign our forehead, lips and heart. Our *mind* that it may take in the holy message, our *lips* that they may ever profess the Gospel, our *heart* that it may preserve the word of life and permit it to yield fruit a hundredfold.

"In *illo* tempore . . . at *that* time." At what time? In the year 33? Yes, but also in the year 1933, and . . . 1944. "At that time," that is, "today," Jesus says to His disciples — to you, to me: "You are the salt of the earth, you are the light of the world." It is in this spirit and with this meaning that we must receive the holy Gospel. When, for example, on the Fifteenth Sunday after Pentecost we hear the Gospel of the "Widow of Naim" we must take it not only *historically* (as it occurred 1900 years ago) but also *liturgically* (as it is happening now). Today Mother Church brings her dead (or crippled) children to the compassionate Jesus who by His life-restoring, life-perfecting mysteries will heal these sons and daughters and give them back to their Mother, the Church, turning her sadness into gladness. Weep not, good Woman, here is your son, your daughter, restored to life!

The Gospel (chanted or read in Holy Mass) is not only *instruction*, it is also *revelation*. In *human* form the *divine* becomes present. As often as the holy Gospel is announced, Christ the Lord steps into our midst. "Jesus in the midst of His disciples!" If the Gospel were instruction only, the frequent repetition of certain Gospel-portions might be considered unnecessary. But because it is an appearance of Christ, a revelation of the Lord, an "epiphany" of our God-King, it is as refreshing as the daily rising sun, old yet ever new. No matter how often a passage be read (*liturgically*, not just privately), no matter how well we might know its contents, it is for us another opportunity to say: Gloria Tibi! Laus Tibi! to Christ our Lord again becoming present in our midst.

3. THE SERMON. THE HOLY GHOST SPEAKS

Epistle, Gospel, Sermon, these three. The sermon is an integral part of the Mass. The *early* Church would not separate Christ the *Highpriest* and Christ the *Teacher*. Whenever she unfolded the "mystery of the Bread and Wine" she also unfolded the "mystery of the Book." A sermon, a homily, was given to the "circumstantes," those "standing about the altar." Should we not welcome the restoration of a thousand years' old practice of the Church? However, the movement today would seem rather *away* from the sermon. The (oft unnecessary) multiplication of Sunday Masses has not been too favorable towards the sermon. But "faith comes by hearing." In not a few places the sermon is dropped altogether during (and because of) the "hot season." I believe, it was quite "hot" when our Lord preached His converting sermon to the woman at Jacob's well. It doesn't make good sense to remove the "warning signal" at a time when temptations for many people are more than ordinary.

Back, therefore, to the sermon; back to a well prepared sermon, also during the summer months. Let it be brief, but let it be! We priests must be good Samaritans who pour the healing oil of God's word into the flock, wounded so often by the robbers of Christian living, wounded so frequently by the robbers of purity and modesty, who during the "hot season" usually strike harder than at any other time. Here at "Holy Cross" we have a daily five to seven minutes homily, also during the summer vacation, at the 8:00 A. M. Mass (the children's Mass). The homily is based on the Mass-text, or the saint "of the day." In so doing we endeavor to show our flock the "eucharistic-moral way" according to the mind of the Church. This 8:00 A. M. celebration is a dialogue Mass or, on higher days, a chanted Mass. Not so long ago, when speaking to a group of religion teachers, about our daily dialogue Mass with brief homily, one of them replied: "But aren't you losing quite a bit of school time?" Losing "time" in the celebration of the mystery of "eternity"! What is education anyway? "Not from bread alone does man live but . . ." The dialogue Mass with homily, and communion of a fairly large group of children and adults, lasts about thirty-five to forty minutes. Our slogan is: "Our school begins daily at 8:00 A. M. before God's altar." Twice a year we remind our people of this slogan. And it works well.

The following homily, "on the eighth Sunday after Pentecost" might serve as a pattern for homiletic preaching "on the Mass-text" (please, consult the respective Mass-text).

"Great is the Lord, and exceedingly to be praised,
in the city of our God, in His holy mountain" (Introit).

Brothers and Sisters in Christ:

INTROIT: We are assembled here to receive in the midst of God's temple His mercy, the incarnate mercy of God. The right hand of the Lord is indeed full of justice. For He spared not His Only-begotten but, in order to redeem the slave, gave up His own Son. O, how great is our God, and exceedingly to be praised in the midst of His city (this church), in His holy mountain (this altar).

COLLECT: We pray this morning with the whole Church. "Give us the spirit to think and do what is right." We are Christians, other Christs. The same mind which is in Christ Jesus must also be in us. We cannot afford to live according to the flesh, and thus fall back into the old bondage.

EPISTLE: We are led by the Spirit. We are His temples. Sons of God we are, privileged to call Him "Abba, Father." Heirs of God we are and joint-heirs with Christ. Alleluja, Great is the Lord and exceedingly to be praised, here in His house, here on this holy altar!

GOSPEL: Through baptism we became stewards of a "rich man" who entrusted heavenly goods to us. So often we have wasted our Master's goods. We have done so again, in some measure at least, during the past week. But this morning we may take the pen of sorrow, dip it into the saving Blood of our great Brother, and strike out the debt we have contracted.

OFFERTORY: For we know that an humble and contrite heart God will not despise. "Thou wilt save the humble people and wilt bring down the eyes of the proud." With an humble heart we bring our gifts to Thy altar, O God.

SECRET: Receive them, Lord, and by the power of Thy grace, may the eucharistic mystery now sanctify our lives here on earth, and help us to reach the joys of eternity. All I am, and all I have, I carry into the life-giving Sacrifice of Christ; my joys and sorrows, my successes and failures. May all redound to Thy greater glory, O God, "through Him and with Him and in Him."

COMMUNION: Then, as we approach the holy Table, we will again "taste and see that the Lord is sweet."

POST-COM: May Thy holy Body and Blood heal us in soul and body, and may we ever feel within us, especially during this new week, the power of the sacrament we now celebrate. Surely, Great is the Lord, and exceedingly to be praised, in the city of our God, in His holy mountain.

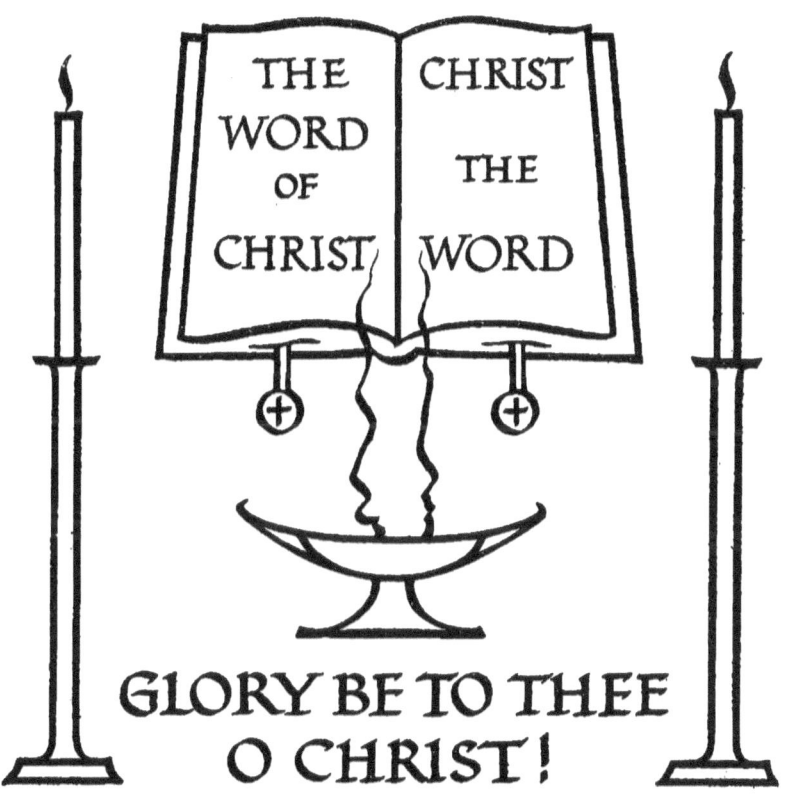

Part Two

THE SACRIFICE-MASS

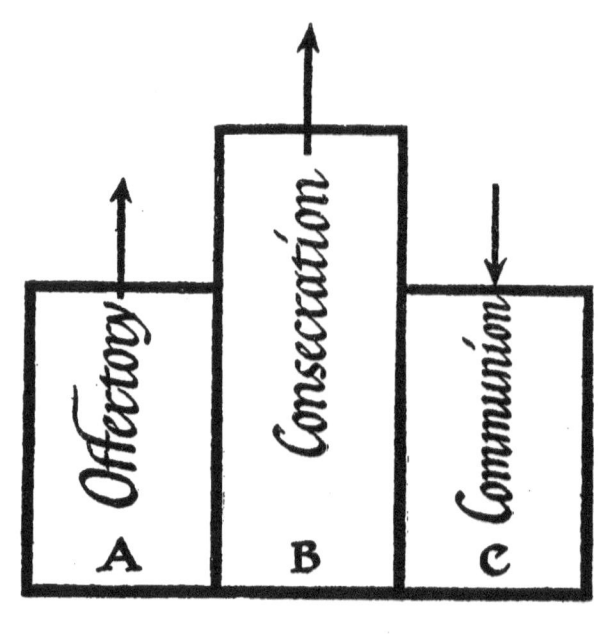

CHAPTER THREE

PART II. THE SACRIFICE-MASS

WE have completed Part I, the *Fore-Mass*. Let us now give our attention to Part II, the *Sacrifice-Mass*. Between the two, however, is a bridge, the *Credo*. We remember how in the Kyrie we called on Father, Son and Holy Spirit, and how from each divine Person we received an answer, in the Epistle, Gospel, Sermon. The Credo is the solemn assurance to the Blessed Trinity that "I believe" 1. in God, the Father Almighty; 2. in Jesus Christ, His only Son our Lord, and 3. in the Holy Ghost, the Lord and Lifegiver. Over this profession of Christian Faith we walk from the vestibule of the *Fore-Mass* into the Sanctuary of the *Sacrifice-Mass*, the "Mystery of Faith."

A. OFFERTORY

"Offertorium, offere," i. e. "the bringing up" of gifts to God. Writes Father Busch: "The faithful of those days (A.D. 300-1100) understood well that they all partook both in the offering of the Mass and in the receiving of the Eucharist, both in sacrifice-oblation and in sacrifice-banquet. The ancient ceremonial brought this out very plainly. The faithful approached the altar at the Offertory and at the Communion, first to give and later to receive. The Mass was both their gift to God through Christ, and God's gift to them through Christ" (*Orate Fratres* vol. II, No. 5).

After the sermon the Christians of old proceeded towards the altar to offer *bread* and *wine* and *themselves* to God, the Father. But not only bread and wine, also flowers, particularly red roses and white lilies, symbols of the two sublime states in the Church: Martyrdom and Virginity. Also gold, silver, clothes, money and whatever else they possessed. Bread and wine first for the divine Head, but also for His members, the clergy and faithful, especially the poor—the "pedes Christi" (the feet of Christ), as the early Church loved to designate the poor. "Whatsoever you do to the *least* of My brethren ("the feet") you do unto Me ("the Head"). The spirit of the offerers was this: "The heart must hold even more than the hands can carry." Behind the *material* gift must stand the *spiritual* oblation. Roughly speaking, after the first thousand years a decided change occurred. The first millennium *spoke less* and *did more*, the second *speaks more* and *does less*. The external form has changed indeed, but the spirit must never change if our Offertory is to be acceptable to God. "It is the *spirit* that quickeneth."

The disappearance of the old Offertory procession certainly was a great loss. Man, made up of spirit and *matter*, had no longer an appropriate *material* gift whereby to express his inward oblation, with the result that the idea of self-oblation grew weaker and weaker. But, thanks to God, we still have an Offertory procession at the ordination of priests and the consecration of a bishop. What a significant moment when the newly ordained priests —"you are the light of the world"— place into the apostolic hands of the ordaining prelate the lighted candle, dedicating themselves by this symbolic act to the work of leading men from darkness into the wonderful light of God and lifting up those already in the light to still brighter glory in Christ, the Light. More solemn than the Offertory by the new priest is that by the new bishop who offers two large candles, and bread and wine for the first sacrifice to be offered by His highpriestly hands. "Behold a great priest who in his days pleased God!" But what a pity that this sublime and divine act is often called a "ceremony," alas, not only "called" thus, but actually treated as such by having the two loaves of bread painted with aluminum and gold-bronze.

In many European parishes the Offertory procession is still observed in Requiem Masses. Well do I remember, how, as a boy of seven or eight, I took part in the Offertory procession around the altar before which we deposited our (money) gifts. Quite suddenly the custom of the procession by the congregation was abandoned —I don't know why — only the sexton continued to make it. This fellow had heavy black hair and wore a loose black cassock (no surplice) and black gloves. The only bright spot in the scene was his face. And then just as abruptly things changed back. A new pastor had come to our parish, a man of fifty, graced with a remarkable liturgical sense. One of the first things he abolished was the "sexton-only-procession." He explained to his people the meaning of the Offertory procession and asked them to take part in it. Which they did. What a joy for us boys when we could march again in the Offertory procession. From now on we also liked our sexton a little better. The program of this new pastor was: Active, soulful participation by the congregation in the Mass and the prayers and chants of the Church, a program all the more significant because it antedated by some four years the liturgical reforms of the sainted Pius X. I may add here that, next to the grace of God and the liturgical sense of my parents, I owe, whatever love for the sacred liturgy I may have, to this grand old pastor.

"When was the Offertory procession abolished," you ask? . . . I answer: "It never was." Haven't we in every parish the world over the so-called Offertory collection? Perhaps most of us do not stop to consider why it is taken up precisely at the Offertory. Our Offertory collection today is the crippled remnant of the erstwhile grand, moving procession of old and young who brought their personal offering of bread and wine, elements that sustain life, symbols therefore of all our life, gifts expressing our inward offering of self and, by the Lord's own choice, the elements which are to be changed into His eucharistic Body and Blood. Our present-day Offertory collection is not very poetic. Ushers with long sticks going through the aisles, holding wire baskets before people's faces, sometimes knocking prayerbooks out of their hands, (certain people seem particularly "devout" during the time of collecting), then carrying the baskets to *some corner* near a side altar where they remain till after service, or whence some "authorized" person will immediately take them to the sacristy to count audibly — during the silence of the canon — the "sacrifices and gifts of Thy people," often to the wonderment and annoyance of the faithful,— all that is not very inspiring.

We today need to restore the liturgical understanding of the offertory collection for the sake of a better appreciation of the entire Mass as an oblation, a sacrifice offered not by Christ alone, nor by the priest alone, but by the entire Christian body-made-one-in-Christ. Is it not true that the majority of our people are not so convinced that their Sunday offering is the *outward* symbol of their *inner* oblation to God? Our offertory-collection is in need of a lifting from the valley of routine, reluctant "money-dumping" to the mountain of conscious, joyful "soul-oblation" expressed in a visible way.

May we not hope that, as a result of the fast growing dogmatic-liturgical restoration the world over, the Church's authorities will invite the faithful to return to the offertory procession as practiced in the Church for twelve or thirteen centuries. John Burchard of Strasbourg, papal master of ceremonies, published in 1502 the following regulations: "In case there are any who wish to offer, the celebrant goes to the epistle side; standing there with head uncovered, he takes off the maniple from his left arm and holding it in his right hand, he offers the end of it to be kissed by all who offer, saying to each: May your sacrifice be acceptable to God, or, May you receive an hundredfold and possess eternal life." As late as 1536 the Council of Cologne ordered "that all the faithful are *bound* to offer on Christmas, Easter, the feast of the Patron Saint, Pentecost and the Assumption of Our Lady."

It is of interest to note that a number of the German bishops, because Catholic *public* charity drives were forbidden by the Hitler government, requested their flocks to make the offering of their gifts for the poor during Holy Mass. A Christmas letter from a friend in Freiburg (Archbishop Groeber's diocese) written in 1937 contained the following information: "On Gaudete Sunday we had a unique experience in our parish church (St. Martin's). Some 800 parishioners carried to the altar their Christmas gifts for the poor. It was touching to see the joy with which the people performed this act of charity and the happiness they experienced as their gifts mounted higher and higher on each side of the altar. How much more elevating is *this* way of giving to the poor than the old way of going from house to house gathering donations by means of a tin-box. We brought our gifts to our Christmas-King who sanctified them and gave them back to His beloved poor."

But, let us remember, whether our gifts are actually carried up to the altar or not, certain it is that the bread and wine on the altar *are the gifts of the faithful assembled,* as nearly every Secret prayer indicates. "Receive, O Lord, the *oblations* and prayers of Thy people." The elements on the altar are the visible symbols of the united brotherhood of all the faithful here assembled before the Lord of heaven and earth.

Now a word about our altarbreads. First of all, would it not be more appropriate to say "bread" instead of "host"? True, the first of the offertory prayers does use the expression, "host," "Receive this immaculate host . . . ," not because it is already "the immaculate host" but because this very bread now presented to God will soon be offered to Him as "immaculate Host" (hostia, victim! "O salutaris Hostia!"). A former Protestant minister once asked me: "Why do you always say 'host,' why don't you say 'altarbread'?"

And then, are not our altarbreads today rather small and thin? Those used in Rome for both priest and people are decidedly larger. Some people would seem to have scruples about larger and thicker breads, fearing lest the recipients might "touch them with their teeth." But what did our Lord say? "Take ye and *eat*, or take ye and let it *melt*?" Surely, we have not forgotten the old axiom: "Nil in intellectu nisi prius fuerit in sensu, nothing can be in our mind which previously has not been in our senses." Is not the smallness and thinness of the eucharistic species apt to lessen in the minds of the people that fuller appreciation of the "Bread of the Strong and the Wine that bringeth forth Virgins?"

In the basement of "Holy Cross" rectory we found an altar-bread iron, so old that it may have come down from the days of Duke St. Wenceslaus who with his own hands prepared the bread and wine for the eucharistic Sacrifice. The housekeeper, following this Saint's example, is now baking with it the large altarbread (for the priest) using one-half "whole-wheat" flour. Everybody seems to be much concerned about the "purity" of the Mass *wine*, but seldom do we hear a doubt expressed about the purity and fitness of the Mass *bread*. When we hear of all the bleaching-processes which flour now-a-days must endure, one wonders if we really have "bread" or some kind of "starch-product." Not so long ago I was told that a certain institution is making altarbreads from flour which is sub-jected to — I don't know how many — chemical bleaching and separating processes. From the "separated" substance the members of that institution bake a "very wholesome table bread" which visitors buy and take home because "it is so very good." But, why in the world, not make use of that very "separated" substance to prepare the bread which is to become the "Bread that containeth all sweetness"?

The offering of bread and wine, money and ourselves, the kind of flour to be used and the size of the altarbread are questions that deserve our earnest attention. Recently a priest friend sent me the following note: "I express to you my sincere gratitude for your con-genial note as well as for your kindness in sending to me a supply of the whole wheat altarbreads. I have used them and it is the first time in my priestly career that I have been able to do so. Like you, I wish that some community would take up the work of making and advocating real altarbreads. Should we tamper with the wine used for sacrifice purposes in the manner in which we tamper with the flour used in making altarbreads I fear that at least some members of the hierarchy would be — and rightly so — up in arms." Where is the community that will make the start?

During the first thousand years we had only one offertory prayer, the Secret. Little was spoken, much was done at the Offertory in those days. The faithful brought up their gifts, chanting an appropriate psalm. It is quite interesting to make a study of the "Offertory verse," the "frame-chant" surrounding the psalm which formerly was sung during the procession of the offerers. In these verses you will find constant references to *spirit, hands, feet, light*, etc., a forceful reminder that our offering to God must not be a thoughtless, mechanical thing, but worship "in spirit and in truth." During the past eight or nine hundred years some *six* prayers have been added to the offertory. As the "doing" decreased the "speaking" increased. Nevertheless these prayers portray strikingly the spirit that must fill our soul at the Offertory. From time to time we should meditate on these prayers. How very "Catholic," all-embracing, is the "Suscipe, Receive, Holy Father . . . ," and how profound and majestic the "Deus qui humanæ . . . ," the prayer for the mingling of wine and water. A wonderful moment, this mingling of wine and water! Christ is the "precious Wine," we the "ordinary water." He, the author of all blessings, may not be blessed. We, in need of redemption, are blessed. The water is drawn into the wine, is lost in it. Our souls are restless until they are "lost" in Christ, until we are "sharers of the divine nature" (St. Peter). "He has become sharer in our humanity that we might become sharers in His divinity."

At the High Mass God's *gifts*, God's *altar*, God's *priest* and God's *people* are incensed. Again we shall let Romano Guardini speak:

"And I saw . . . and an angel came, and stood before the altar, having a golden censer. And there was given him much incense . . . And the smoke of the incense of the prayers of the saints ascended up before God, from the hand of the angel." So says St. John in the Apocalypse.

"There is a grand beauty in this laying of the bright grains on the glowing coal and then the scented smoke rising from the swinging censer. It is like a melody with rhythmic movement and sweet odor. Without any purpose, as clear as a song. A gift of unreserving love.

"So once, when the Lord sat at table in Bethany, and Mary brought the costly spikenard and poured it over His feet, and dried them with her hair, and the house was filled with odor, narrow minds murmured: 'To what purpose is this waste?' The Son of

God replied: 'Let her alone, she hath done it for my burial.' A mystery of death were here, of love, of odor, of sacrifice.

"And all that is in the incense: a mystery of beauty that knows of no purpose — it only mounts up: love that burns and consumes itself and passes in death. And does the barren mind stand here also asking: To what purpose?

"A sacrifice of sweet odor; and Scripture itself says: These are the prayers of the Saints. Incense is a symbol of prayer, and precisely of that prayer that knows no purpose — that asks for nothing, but rises up like the Gloria at the end of a Psalm — that desires only to adore and thank God 'because of His great Glory.'

".... The more intense love, the greater the sacrifice: and the odor comes from the consuming fire."

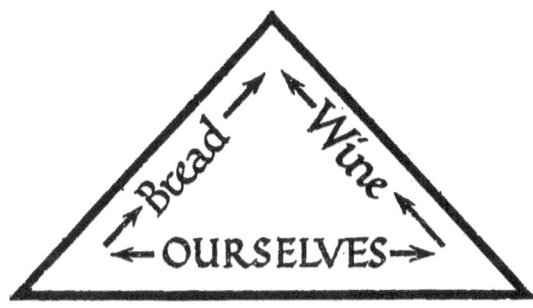

Bread, wine and ourselves. And these THREE must be ONE. Only then will there be a real offertory, one that is acceptable to the most Holy Trinity. "Receive, O most Holy Trinity this oblation." The more sincerely and soulfully we make this oblation, the more it will redound "to the praise and glory of God's name, to our own benefit, and to that of all His holy Church."

CHAPTER FOUR

B. Canon and Consecration

With the "per omnia sæcula sæculorum" of the celebrant, and the "Amen" of the faithful, the Offertory comes to an end. By their consenting "So be it," "the holy people of God" seal the action of the anointed "servant of God" at the altar. Our Catholic people must again become conscious of their sharing in Christ's priesthood. There is the "special" priesthood conferred by the sacrament of Holy Orders and the "general" priesthood bestowed by the sacraments of baptism and confirmation. When speaking to children about the *special* and *general* priesthood I love to make use of thumb, index and middle fingers; the "small one," the "higher one" and the "highest one." Distinct, indeed, from one another, yet united by the same bond of flesh and blood. So it is with the wonderful outpouring of Christ's Priesthood. A smaller portion, as it were, is given in Baptism, a larger one in Confirmation and a still greater one in Holy Orders. Baptism and Comfirmation imprint a sacred character concerning which St. Thomas says that "it is a certain participation in the priesthood of Christ." We are a priestly family, "a chosen generation, a kingly people," bound together by a mystic blood-relationship with Christ our Highpriest, through the sacraments of Baptism — Confirmation — Holy Orders. At no time is this *special* and *general* priesthood so perfectly exercised as in the great Sacrifice of Christ-with-His-redeemed-flock in which He with us, and we "through Him, with Him and in Him" give all honor and glory to God.

The Offertory is over. And yet it is not over. It was only the beginning of an oblation which "through Him and with Him and in Him" will ripen into a perfect Sacrifice, an oblation worthy of the majesty of that great God before whom the angels tremble, the powers stand in awe, the seraphim and cherubim cry out unceasingly: "Holy, Holy, Holy is the Lord God of sabaoth." Had we no more to offer than a little bread, a little wine and our own little selves we could indeed exclaim with St. Peter: "Lord we have labored all night . . . all during Mass . . . and have caught nothing."

Thanks be to God, we have *One* who is able to make our oblation truly worthy of God, One who will turn the bread into His sacrificial Body, the wine into His sacrificial Blood and ourselves unto Himself. "When I shall be lifted up I will draw all things unto Myself."

The moment of that great change draws nigh. Therefore, "Sursum corda!" Lift up your hearts! "Gratias agamus (eucharistæsomen) Domino Deo nostro." Let us celebrate the Eucharist to the Lord our God! The Preface leads us into the Holy of Holies where we shall give thanks (gratias *agere*, "do" thanks) to God "through Christ our Lord." In union with the heavenly choirs we fall down before the Lord God and exclaim: "Sanctus, sanctus, sanctus," and, joining the apostles, disciples and children of the first Palm Sunday, we welcome with palms of love the King of Peace who is about to enter into the city of His eucharistic Jerusalem: "Blessed is He who cometh in the name of the Lord. Hosanna in the highest!"

THE VENERABLE CANON

"TE igitur . . ." Words and actions of overwhelming significance! With eyes directed to heaven, his hands raised . . . folded . . . extended and then laid outstretched on the altar — like Christ's hands on the Cross — the celebrant kisses the holy Altar and "through Jesus Christ our Lord" (without whom no man can come to the Father) he beseeches the "most merciful Father to bless these gifts, these offerings, these holy and unspotted sacrifices." An act of perfect submission, not unlike that great humbling of the Highpriest who in perfect submission to the will of the Father "became obedient unto death."

Artists of bye-gone ages, realizing the lapidarian force of these opening words of the Canon have given expression to their inspiration by illuminating in colors and gold the initial letter "T"— the "Cross-letter." As time went on the illumination of the letter "T" turned into a "crucifixion group," which gradually became so large that a whole page was devoted to it. That accounts for the full page picture inserted between Preface and Canon, unfortunately putting asunder what in former days had been united.

MEMENTO OF THE CHURCH (1)

a) "For Thy holy Catholic Church," Christ's Bride and Body, in order that God would 1. grant her peace, 2. protect, 3. unite and 4.

govern her *throughout the world.* A magnificent prayer for peace, world-peace, offered daily;

b) "together with (una cum) Thy servant Pius," in whom is vested all power, from whom every priest derives his power, and with whom alone he may rightfully offer the Sacrifice of the New Law;

c) "and our Bishop N.," the highpriest, shepherd and father of the diocese;

d) "And all true believers and promoters (bishops, priests, missionaries, lay-apostles) of the Catholic and apostolic faith."

MEMENTO OF THE LIVING (2)

"Formerly," says *St. Andrew's Missal,* "the priest used to read from tablets or diptychs the names of the living or dead who were to be specially remembered." "Strange but true," during a service witnessed in an Episcopalian church in New York, the "priest" turned at this part of the "Mass" and read some twelve names of benefactors of the congregation. We Catholics "wouldn't have time for that kind of stuff." Besides, such public mementoes would "disturb" some people who "must make their novena to Saint so-and-so" while the "King of all the Saints" is proclaiming from His altar the royal manifesto of mankind's redemption. The celebrant prays:

a) "For God's servants and handmaids N.N."

b) "For all here present whose faith and devotion (sacrifice-mindedness) are known to God, for whom we offer, or who offer up to God this Sacrifice of praise for themselves and all those dear to them . . ."

All, those present and absent, the entire family of God, must share in the blessings of this Sacrifice and obtain the fulfillment of their desires.

MEMENTO OF THE SAINTS (3)

Now the Saints of God, our triumphant brethren, are invited to join us in the procession up the mystic Calvary. Here they come, under the leadership of "the glorious ever Virgin Mary, Mother of God," two by two, the glorious Apostles of the Church, Peter and Paul, Andrew and James and the other members of the apostolic college; then twelve of Christ's blood-witnesses who are particularly dear to the Roman church, Linus and Cletus, Clement and Sixtus . . . Cosmas and Damian; finally that great multitude which no man can number, from all tribes and languages and peoples. All must accompany us to God's altar and, by their merits and prayers, help us to be defended in all things and to enjoy God's continuous protection.

(Hanc igitur. Quam oblationem.)

Says *St. Andrew's Missal:* "The priest spreads his hands over chalice and host (bread!) as the highpriest formerly did over the victim sacrificed in expiation for the sins of the people ..." Surely, that significant action of the old Jewish highpriest must come to our mind as we say: "This oblation of our service and that of Thy whole family, we beseech Thee, graciously accept." But is there not yet another and deeper meaning to this spreading of the priest's hands over the gifts? I am thinking of the "imposition of hands" which takes place in the administration of *every* sacrament. In Baptism the priest extends hands over the catechumen. In Confirmation the bishop imposes his hand on the confirmandus. In Penance the confessor extends his right hand over the contrite penitent. In Extreme Unction the ritual lets the priest pray: "By the imposition of my hands." In Holy Orders the imposed hands of the bishop raise the deacon to Christ's eternal priesthood. In Matrimony husband and wife with joined hands administer to one another the "great sacrament."

And so also here in the confecting of the "SACRAMENT of all sacraments" the priest's hands are extended over the bread and wine about to be transubstantiated. Priestly hands, power-laden hands, hands holding gifts as they turn from an earthly into a heavenly substance, from life-less bread into the Bread of Life, from an insignificant portion of wine into the price of our redemption. Let us again listen to Romano Guardini:

"The whole body is the tool and the expression of the soul. The soul does not merely dwell in the body, as if it were a house, but it lives and works in every member and every fibre. It speaks in every line, and form, and movement of the body. But in a very special way the face and the hands are the tool and the mirror of the soul.

"This is obvious with regard to the face. But watch anyone — yourself — and see how a movement of temper, of joy, of astonishment, of expectation is revealed by the hand. How often a quick raising or a slight twitch of the hand says more even than a spoken word. It speaks sometimes as if a spoken word were almost coarse compared with the delicate language of the hand, which tells so much.

"After the face, the hand is the most spiritual part of the body. It is truly firm and strong, as the tool for work, as the weapon for attack or defense; but it is very delicately formed, with many joints, flexible and penetrated with sensitive nerves of feeling. It is truly a machine through which man can reveal his soul. By the hand we welcome the stranger and join souls when we join hands — and with this act we express trust, joy, agreement, sympathy.

"So we cannot think that the hand will be without its language when the soul has so much to say and to receive in God's presence, when it desires to give itself to God and to welcome Him in prayer.

"When we wish to gather ourselves together alone with God, then one hand firmly clasps the other, finger folds on finger, so that, as it were, the inner current, which might flow out, may be conducted from hand to hand, and thus return within, so that all may remain inside with God. It is a gathering together, a recollection of oneself; staying at home with the hidden God. It says: 'God is mine, I am His, and we are alone together within.'

"So again, if there is an inner distress, a great need, a great pain which threatens to break out. Again, hand locks in hand, and thus holds in the soul, until it forces it into calm.

"But if anyone stands in a humble, reverent attitude before God, then the outstretched hands meet flat with each other. That speaks of firm control, of overmastering homage. It is a humble, well-ordered telling of our own mind, and an attentive, ready hearing of God's word. Or it tells of dedication, of giving ourselves, as if the hands, with which we defend ourselves, were placed, bound, in the Hands of God.

"Frequently the soul lays itself entirely open before God, in great happiness or thanksgiving. Like an organ, it opens its whole register, and the fullness within flows to God. Then a man parts his hands and lifts them wide open, so that the stream from the soul may flow freely, and the soul may fully receive what it thirsts for.

"Lastly, it may happen that he wishes to give himself to God in complete dedication with all that is in him, all that he is and all that he has, knowingly offering himself as a victim for sacrifice. Then he draws in his arms and hands, and folds them crosswise on his breast.

"Beautifully and greatly do the hands speak. Of them the Church says that God has given them to us, in order that we may 'carry our souls in them.'

"Take, therefore, this holy language in earnest. God listens to it. It speaks from the innermost soul. It can also speak of sloth of heart, of distraction and of failings. Hold your hands rightly, and be careful that the outer and the inner truly respond to each other.

"It is a delicate matter of which we have been speaking. It is not a subject to be lightly talked about. We shrink from it unconsciously.

"So much the more careful we must be to keep to the right way. We must not make of it an idle, artistic play; but it must speak for us, so that in every truth the body may say to God what the soul means."

Here is a practical point for priests and people. "Familiarity breeds contempt," they say. Let us put it this way: Familiarity is apt to beget slovenliness, soul-lessness. We do things daily, do them over and over again, do them mechanically. We make signs of the cross, we greet the flock "Dominus vobiscum," but feel perhaps no longer the Christ-power in these holy signs and words. "Eyes they have and see not, ears they have and hear not," said the Psalmist. Isn't it true? Again and again we must pull ourselves together and rise, lest human frailty will chill the precious things of God. Beautiful souls will do the beautiful things of God in a beautiful way!

The "Quam oblationem" follows, the petition that God "make worthy and acceptable" the oblation which human weakness has prepared for the God of strength, so that "it may become *for us* the Body and Blood of His most beloved Son, our Lord Jesus Christ." And now, a few moments more, and heaven and earth will embrace each other on the holy Altar.

"Qui Pridie" (The Efficacious Narrative) (6)

"Who the day before He suffered . . ." commences the sacred story, a story which effects what it tells. ". . . Take ye, and eat ye all of this, For This Is My Body." Bread of earth is become the Bread of heaven, His Flesh for the life of the world, the sacrificed Body and Blood of the Highpriest and Good Shepherd. "In like manner . . . ," as on the great Thursday, the few drops of wine are turned into the gigantic stream of Christ's Blood, "of which a single drop, for sinners spilt, can purge the entire world from all its guilt."

"As often as you shall do these things ye shall do them in remembrance of Me." Now they are being *done* again. The Sacrifice of Calvary is re-presented, rendered present. Christ the Highpriest places His one Sacrifice, the world-redeeming Sacrifice of the new and unending Testament, into our hands as our perfect Sacrifice to God the Father. The Cross-oblation of the immortal and glorified Christ, "the Lamb, as if slain," is now on our Altar.

The "Anamnesis" (Calling to Mind). "Unde et Memores" (1)

"Do this in remembrance of Me." Faithful to the Lord's command "we, *Thy servants* and *Thy holy people* are mindful of the blessed *Passion*, the *Resurrection* from the dead and the glorious *Ascension* of Christ Thy Son." Yes, priests *and* people are *mindful* of the *whole* work of redemption which has again become present on the altar. That of which we now are (subjectively) mindful lies (objectively) before us. (a) We are mindful of the great things now on the Altar, (b) the great things now on the altar fill our mind. The two together constitute the *"memory* of Christ"; the *"Do* this in *remembrance* of Me." "For as often as this saving Victim is offered up, so often is enacted the whole work of redemption" (secret, Ninth Sunday after Pentecost). Centuries ago the Epiphany and Parousia (the *beginning* and *completion* of the work of redemption) also were added. The whole work of redemption, of which the Lord's Sacrifice on the Cross is climax and center, is now offered to the Father.

"After the consecration has made present the Body and Blood of Christ on the altar" (writes Father Dahmus in a splendid article in the September 1943 issue of *The Ecclesiastical Review*) "the celebrant and the holy people of God perform the great liturgical act of offering the Body and Blood to the Father." "We offer to Thy most excellent majesty of Thy gifts and presents, a pure Victim, a holy Victim, an immaculate Victim, the holy Bread of eternal life and the Chalice of everlasting salvation." In other words, consecration provides the Sacrifice, which, between consecration and the 'Pater noster,' we (priest *and* people) offer up to the Father in heaven. The venerable practice in many Benedictine monasteries of ringing the bell during this 'time of offering' deserves universal imitation.

"SUPRA QUAE" AND "SUPPLICES" (2 AND 3)

". . . accept them as Thou wert pleased to accept the gifts of Thy just servant *Abel*, and the sacrifice of our patriarch *Abraham*, and that which Thy highpriest *Melchisedech* offered . . ." Why these three, why not others out of the numberless sacrifices of the Old Law? Because of their special relation to the *Passion*, *Resurrection* and *Ascension* spoken of in the previous prayer (Unde et memores).

1. PASSION: Abel, the symbol of Christ slain by His own whose Blood cries to heaven for . . . mercy.

2. RESURRECTION: Abraham whose only-begotten was offered, and then given back 'alive.'

— 55 —

3. ASCENSION: Melchisedech, the symbol of Christ, the Highpriest "according to the order of Melchisedech" who came "without geneology," offered the "clean oblation" and *returned* whence he came.

Bowing low the priest says: "Supplices, we most humbly beseech Thee, command these things to be carried up by the hands of Thy holy angel to Thine altar on high . . ." How much need is there for such a petition? Does not Christ, the Lamb, standing on the heavenly Altar perpetually present to the Father the sacrifice He offered on Calvary? Indeed. But are not *we* also part and parcel of this Sacrifice? To express it mathematically: Christ Jesus the *Head* plus the Church His *Body* plus we His *members* are *one* great oblation. Surely then, there is need that the Sacrifice also of the Church and her members which day after day is offered anew be carried to the heavenly Altar. "In this act of sacrifice" says Pope Pius XII (*Mystici Corporis*) "through the hands of the priest, whose word alone has brought the Immaculate Lamb to be present on the altar, the faithful themselves with one desire and one prayer offer It to the eternal Father,— the most acceptable Victim of praise and propitiation for the Church's universal needs. And just as the Divine Redeemer, dying on the Cross, offered Himself as Head of the whole human race to the eternal Father, so "in this pure oblation" He offers not only Himself as Head of the Church to the heavenly Father, but in Himself His mystical members as well. He embraces them all, even the weak and ailing, in the tenderest love of His Heart."

The Head offers Himself with His members, and the members are privileged to offer Him and "through Him, with Him and in Him" themselves "so that all who from *this* participation of the Altar (altar stands for sacrifice) will receive the most sacred Body and Blood of Thy Son, may be filled with every heavenly blessing and grace."

Here we should like to ask two questions:

1. Why do nearly all of our English (and German) missals translate "ex hac altaris participatione" with "by participation at this altar"? Surely, the ablative "hac" does not belong to the genitive "altaris."

2. Is it really ideal to give holy Communion on any day, especially on the Lord's day and the greater feasts of redemption, "ex *ulla* participatione (from *that* participation)," instead of "ex *hac* participatione (from *this* participation)"? The need of liturgical orientation was brought home to me some five years ago when

I saw how an ordaining prelate was compelled to open the tabernacle to communicate the newly ordained priests who had indeed con-celebrated and co-consecrated with him but were not permitted to receive "ex *hac* participatione" the fruit of their very *first* Mass.

MEMENTO OF THE DEPARTED (4)

". . . for living and dead" did the celebrant raise the altarbread at the Offertory. And now that this feeble bread has become the Bread of life he prays that it may benefit also those "who are gone before us with the (baptismal) sign of faith" and bring "to all that rest in Christ a place of refreshment, light and peace." Compare this prayer, full of hope and consolation, uttered by the Church (who practically never speaks of "poor" souls) to the, at times, almost gruesome "poor souls" prayers found in many man-made prayerbooks. "To all that *rest in Christ!*"

MEMENTO OF US SINNERS (5)

"Nobis quoque peccatoribus!" Grant us sinners "some part and fellowship" with the citizens of heaven, whose partnership we are experiencing on earth in the celebration of this heaven-and-earth-uniting Sacrifice. Fifteen of these heavenly citizens are mentioned by name, seven *men*-martyrs, seven *women*-martyrs under the leadership of Christ's royal herald, St. John the Baptist. "Admit us into their company, not by virtue of *our* merits, but by *Thy own* free pardon. Through Christ our Lord."

MEMENTO OF ALL NATURE (6)

Bread and wine, roses and lilies, silver and gold, oil and garments which in days of yore the faithful deposited about the altar received their blessing at this particular moment. Even now, on Holy Thursday, the 'oil of the sick' is blessed here. Creation, disfigured by Adam's sin, must be transfigured by Christ's sanctifying Sacrifice. Could inanimate creation speak it would surely chant a 'Jubilate Deo' because some of its elements (bread and wine) have been lifted from a state of weakness into the Holy God, the Strong God, the Immortal God "by whom all things were made" and through whom they are now "sanctified, quickened, blessed and given to us."

THE END OF THE CANON
"Pasa He Doxa"
"All Honor and Glory"

The priest:

1. PER IPSUM: WE, THROUGH HIM
2. ET CUM IPSO: WE, WITH HIM
3. ET IN IPSO: WE, IN HIM

GIVE TO GOD THE FATHER ALMIGHTY
IN THE UNITY OF THE HOLY SPIRIT
ALL HONOR AND GLORY
FOREVER AND EVER

The faithful: AMEN!

All honor and glory! Amen, so be it! Such was the purpose of the Sacrifice of the Cross. Such is the purpose of its re-enactment, the Sacrifice of the Mass.

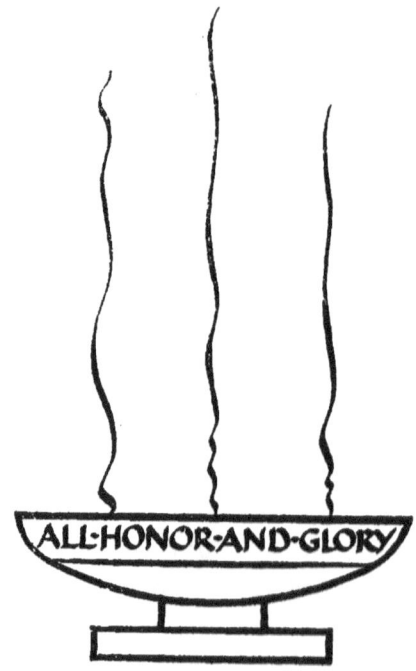

ALL-HONOR-AND-GLORY

CHAPTER FIVE

C. COMMUNION

AT the Offertory we gave to God as much as human limitations permitted us to give. But after Consecration we gave infinitely "through Him and with Him and in Him." What more can one give than "*all* honor and glory"? The *best* there is we gave to our Father.

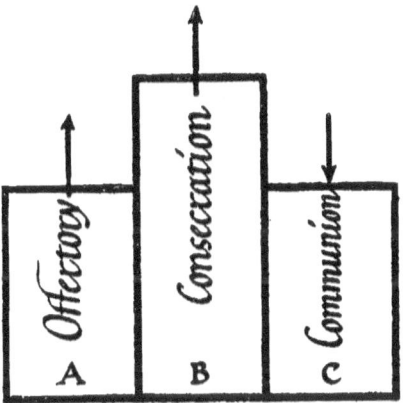

And now the Father invites us to be His table-guests to give the *best* He has to us: The most holy Body and Blood of His sacrificed Son. "Venite, populi, ad sacrum et immortale mysterium, come, ye peoples, to the sacred and immortal mystery," come to the "sacred family-meal (con-vivium) in which Christ is eaten, the memory of His passion is renewed, the inner man is filled with divine life, and a pledge of future glory is given to us" (St. Thomas).

There are three tables which play an important part in man's life and which are very closely related to one another. The *meal-table* in our home, the *altar-table* in our church and the *glory-table* in heaven. At the *first* we pray: "Mensae coelestis participes faciat nos Rex aeternae gloriae, may the King of everlasting glory make us sharers of the heavenly table." At the *second* we "taste and see that the Lord is sweet." This second table sanctifies the first and prepares for the *third* where we experience "what great things God hath prepared for them that love Him."

Before eating we must pray. The meal-prayer ere God's children approach their Father's table is the "Pater noster," the Lord's prayer, the prayer of the Father's Son, the prayer born in the heart of the Eldest Brother on the day when His brethren asked Him: "Lord, teach us to pray!" May God speed the day that will end that awful *mumbling* of the most sacred of all prayers, the "Our Father," heard so often in Catholic parishes. I say "Catholic," because quite frequently our non-Catholic brethren put us to shame by their reverent recitation of the Lord's prayer.

Oremus! (a) Praeceptis salutaribus *moniti* (b) et divina institutione *formati:* so commences the eucharistic table-prayer before communion. Concerning this introduction to the "Our Father" Dr. Franz Mueller in an interesting article written some years ago for the liturgical review *Orate Fratres* arrived at the following conclusions:

(a) During the Fore-Mass we were encouraged by the "praecepta salutaria," the saving doctrines which God infused into our soul, especially through the Epistle and Gospel.

(b) During the Sacrifice-Mass, which is the "divine institution" ('instare', the action *in* which *stands* the 'divine') we were *formed,* were given a new 'form,' the 'form of Christ,' the divine Magnetism of the crucified-glorified Christ having permeated our entire being. By "Word" (in the Fore-Mass) and by "Sacrament" (in the Sacrifice-Mass) we were lifted up, transformed and in a fuller measure made "heirs of God and joint-heirs of Christ," a position and honor that give us a certain right to say: *"Our* Father."

The *"fractio panis"* follows. "He took bread into His hands and *broke* it ... " In his interesting book *'Eucharistia'* Father Kramp, S.J., in a chapter devoted to the "Papal Mass" as celebrated in the 7th and 8th centuries points out how acolytes near the Pope's altar were holding the "eucharistic Leaven" from the previous papal Mass, and how at the "commingling" the sacred Portion from the Sacrifice of *yesterday* was added to *today's*; and how other acolytes carried a Particle of the sacred Bread of the Pope's Mass to each parish priest of the twenty-five Roman Churches who would not continue their Mass until they had received from their Father the "Sign of unity, the Bond of charity, the Sacrament of piety." What a spirit of fellowship! "We, being many, are one bread and one body, all that partake of one bread and of one chalice!"

The "*osculum pacis*". Sometimes one may wonder with how much "soul" the kiss of peace, the kiss of unity and fraternal fellowship is given. We moderns have become rather mechanical and superficial. The shell is there, but often the kernel is wanting. The celebrant kisses the Altar —"the Altar is Christ," says the Roman Pontifical — receives from the Prince of peace the heavenly gift of peace, and passes it on to the flock. "Pax tecum!" Whenever and wherever human beings come together there is apt to be some sort of elbow-rubbing. If your brother has a grudge against you, you had better put down your gift, go and first iron out the difficulties and then bring your gift to the altar. "Et cum spiritu tuo"!

"Peace"! The angels announced it at His humble birth, He Himself announced it on His glorious Easter. "Peace" is the program of His Church. "Peace" wrote the martyr-Christians with joyous enthusiasm on the walls of their subterranean cemeteries. And the great Benedict beholding the collapse of Greco-Roman culture and the arrival of a new order — to be placed on Teutonic shoulders — quickly stretched forth his monastic arm into the depths of the Catacombs, lifted up the "Peace" of ancient Christian Rome and bestowed it as a most precious heritage to those nations "who were poor in which the Romans had been rich, and rich in which the Romans had become poor," so that these *new* carriers of the Christian deposit might enjoy "that Peace of Christ which surpasseth all understanding." Come back to the world, thou heavenly dove, thou peace of Christ! Lamb of God, who takest away the sins of the world, take away all hatred, bloodshed and war. "May the peace of the Lord always be with you!" "Dona nobis pacem, grant us peace," that peace which keeps our minds and hearts *in* Christ Jesus our Lord.

"PANEM coelestem accipiam." With profound humility the celebrant takes first the heavenly Bread . . . then the divine Wine. May they preserve my soul unto life everlasting! After the father of God's family come the children. By Christ's strength all have climbed on the Tree of Sacrifice, now let all eat of the fruit of this Tree of life. No longer are they warned: Stay away from the tree! Eat not of its fruit! For, if you do, you shall die the death. Now they are commanded: Come and eat! For, unless you eat, you shall not have life in you. The tree of malediction has given way to the Tree of Benediction, the fruit of death to the Fruit of Life. "May the Body of our Lord Jesus Christ preserve your soul unto life everlasting. Amen."

"Communion" it is. Union with Christ. Union through Him with one another. Christ and I, Christ and my brother and sister, my brother, sister and I are ONE. Blessed triangle!

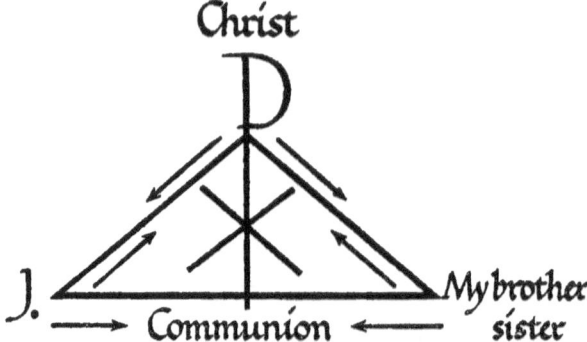

"Ut omnes *unum* sint, that all be *one*" was the great prayer of the Good Shepherd who, because He loved His own unto the end, laid down His life for His sheep, so that "as Thou, Father, in Me, and I in Thee, they also may be *one* in us."

In holy fellowship we offer, in holy fellowship we eat, in holy fellowship we give thanks. "Pour upon us the Spirit of Thy love that Thou mayest make us of one mind whom Thou hast nourished with the *one bread* from heaven."

"Ite, Missa est!" Solemnly the Church dismisses her sanctified sons and daughters. Not with a mechanical, cold: "You can go, the Mass is ended," but with that spirit in which the Lord commissioned His apostles: "Ite, go ye into the whole world!" Ite, so also go you forth as apostles of Christ. Carry the divine fire from the altar into the world, into your home, into your shop, into your fields, into the hearts of men. The late Dr. Stephan of Breslau used to say: "Holy Mass has *three* parts: 1. The Fore-Mass, 2. The Sacrifice-Mass and 3. The Mass through the day."

"Ite!" A sacred commission is this "Ite." In order that we might be able to fulfill it, in order that we might go forth as apostles, as carriers of divine life, love and peace, the priest imparts to us the "blessing of God the Father and the Son and the Holy Ghost."

"Amen," we answer. "So be it!"

THE LAST GOSPEL

The idea of a "second" gospel, and that at the end of a eucharistic service, was foreign to the mind of the infant Church. We may add that perhaps even today this "last gospel" is to be considered not so much as "gospel" but rather as "thanksgiving and consecration to our glorious Highpriest" who offered with us His most holy Sacrifice to the honor of God and the sanctification of His members.

"There was a man sent by God," John, yes, but also you and I, "to give testimony of the light." To give testimony of Christ, the light, is our first business. We are not the light, we are only the lantern of the light. We must decrease. He must increase. In every holy Mass God sends us "to give testimony of the light," testimony by our thoughts, words and actions, testimony by a truly Christian life—a Christian is another Christ,—testimony before the word by "confessing that great name of God's only-begotten Son before the kings and powers of this world" (Palmsunday preface), a testimony that will merit the fulfillment of those awe-inspiring words: "He that shall confess Me before men, him will I confess before My Father who is in heaven."

"The Word was made Flesh" again in the great oblation now coming to a close. "We have (again) seen His glory, the glory of the Only-begotten of the Father, full of grace and truth." With a joyous "Deo gratias, thanks be to God" we conclude the "gratiarum actio," the great "Thanksgiving," and then go forth with Christ living and working in us. "I live, now not I, Christ lives in me." We look at the world, at our work, at our fellowmen with eyes purified and sanctified through the Eucharist; with hearts enkindled by the warmth of the "Lumen Christi, the Light of Christ."

We continue to grow and bear fruit as branches of the Vine; we continue to work for the upbuilding of the Body of Christ "until we all meet unto the unity of faith, and the knowledge of the Son of God, unto a perfect man, unto the measure of the age of the fulness of Christ" (*Eph.* 4, 13), and through Him in the charity of the Holy Spirit unto the Father.

OREMUS! Let us pray!

O God,
who in this wonderful sacrament hast left us
a memorial of Thy passion,

grant us, we beseech Thee so to venerate
the sacred mysteries of Thy Body and Blood,

that we may ever perceive within us the
fruit of Thy redemption.

Who livest and reignest with God the Father,
in the unity of the Holy Spirit, God forever and ever."
Amen.

So be it!

www.ingramcontent.com/pod-product-compliance
Lightning Source LLC
Chambersburg PA
CBHW030328130626
46554CB00011B/1018